FREEDOM FROM FATAL THINKING

God's Remedy for Healing of the Mind

BY
BILLY BURKE

ISBN: 978-1-881189-47-3

Cover & graphic design by Marten's Creative

Published by:
Family Foundations International
P.O. Box 320
Littleton, Colorado 80160

For:
Billy Burke World Outreach
P.O. Box 25441
Tampa, FL 33622

Printed in the United States of America
Reprint in 1998
Reprint in 2000
Reprint in 2010

All Scripture quotations are taken from The New King James Bible unless otherwise noted: *The New King James Bible*, Thomas Nelson Publishers, 1982

DEDICATION

This book is lovingly dedicated to my precious grandmother, "Mam," and to my wonderful mother, both of whom, throughout their lives, have personified the Christian faith. Without their prayers and their unconditional love, I never would have made it.

Thanks, Mam and Mom!

c o n t e n t s

FORWARD

Billy Burke is more than a worker of miracles; he is a man of faith. I have ministered with him in Europe, Canada, and the United States, and I have found his teaching on directing our thoughts positively toward God to be liberating and character-building.

I have been involved with him since the formation of the church in Florida. He has gathered around himself some precious saints who are growing both in grace and in expression of faith in the promises of God.

I challenge you to read this, his first book, with a heart open to God. Let it speak to you until your negative instincts have been controlled by the positive faith Jesus speaks to your heart.

JUDSON CORNWALL

THE THREE GREATEST INFLUENCES

Just about everybody today, in some way, is on a mission to capture a personal healing for themselves. Our world is riddled with diseases and strange sicknesses that have never before been seen on this planet. The HIV virus, the Ebola virus, Legionnaire's disease and the list goes on. Today, the germs, viruses and the bacteria which have hit the airstreams are causing untold heartache and damage worldwide.

People are locked into an emotional prison. There are broken hearts and wounded spirits. Lives are in shambles because of divorce, abortion, desertion and many flavors of dysfunction. The hearts of families are bleeding on the inside spiritually and falling apart, as there is nowhere for sure footing.

Today, people are being racked as voices are speaking into their minds. The results are a high rate of suicide, drug abuse and general deviant behavior. The pressures are tremendous because of trying to match up to a standard that no one can seem to attain, along with the gender crisis of men wanting to be women and women wanting to be men.

There is a financial earthquake looming on the horizon that is causing many to think "Can I ever make enough? Can my family ever be secure?" The mental torment is ravishing the minds of men and removing all peace.

Of course, there is also a deep hunger for spiritual reality. People are looking for any New Age guru or anything that will help them be better, feel better and do better—no holds barred. Everybody is on a mad dash, a search for inner tranquility and emotional strength. They are looking for love and for healing everywhere but in the right places. They are looking for love in all the wrong places. The bookstores will tell you that, books on healing and recovery and restoration are at an all-time high. Yet, a lot of the books that you find on the market don't even have the name of Jesus or the Word of God in them. But, they do have principles, doors, keys and avenues on how to like yourself and how to get in touch with yourself. They will tell you that you have the power within yourself; all you have to do is tap into it.

The television talk shows have become the pulpits of the western world. When people watch these talk shows with the celebrities and other lives that are so messed up, they are searching for answers and for personal resolve. They need a remedy for their hurting world, for their dying bodies, for their riddled minds.

Then, there are the people that seem to be waiting on modern medicine, sitting on the edge of their chairs waiting for the next wonder drug to come on the scene.

There is a vitamin craze. There is a jogging and physical fitness craze. There is a psychic power craze because people today are so desperate, they grasp for straws. They are trying to break out of their house of dysfunction and find some meaning and purpose for their lives. So, you see there is so much, so much, so much heartache.

There is the physical disease, there is the emotional pain, there is the mental torment, but then there is the spiritual hunger.

The spiritual hunger today is causing a turning every which way. Some are turning to the dark side where they call in for telephone sex and have a drink out of the cup of devils and demons with whom they are speaking over the phone. They turn to the bottle and guzzle down alcohol. They think they can drink away their pain and sorrow.

There is gambling where people go to the casinos and back alleys and begin to roll the dice, play craps and take a chance on their cards. Some people are risking literally everything they have on a roll of the dice or the spin of a wheel.

People are desperate! It becomes like a storyline that runs across the front of a person's mind. The characters on the screen aren't fictitious though; they are real. They, themselves, are the characters. The storyline is being generated through thought patterns that can easily be traced. The crime scene becomes our own mind, where attitudes, patterns and behaviors are launched forth. We begin to act out and live out our thought processes. Any psychologist will tell you that, mostly, what people think—they say. Mostly what they say—they do. It is the infamous "think, say and do".

We wake up and realize we have been both a victim of mental rape and a willing participant of passive thinking. We don't protect our eyes and ears, which are the inroads and avenues that deliver all brain food to our minds. Our minds then become polluted with violence, sex and all kinds of compromise that seems to feed the bloody part of man. That is what David said in Psalm 5, there is a bloody and deceitful side to man; and whatever you take in with your eyes affects your whole being. Your eyes and ears are receptors. They are inroads; a conveyor belt, an assembly line that delivers the goods into your mind and stores it, like boxes in a big warehouse.

Once the eyes and ears deliver the goods, then personal thoughts form a thinking process. Your thinking process is formed from all that you see and all that you hear. This is what forms and creates habits and, eventually, a belief system. What your eyes see, what your ears hear and how you receive it, determines the level of freedom or the level of bondage that you find yourself in.

The three greatest influences which impact you in your lifetime are (1) what you see, (2) what you hear, and (3) what you think. What you see and what you hear will often determine what you think. Once you think it, you will usually begin to show it, to speak it and to live it.

In Proverbs, the Bible says, "As a man thinketh in his heart, so is he." Whatever we think in our heart is what we will usually project. Ultimately, it will determine our own self-esteem and our personal value system. That is usually what sets us forth. That is usually what creates our behavior. That is what usually forms habits.

As a man thinketh in his heart about money; as he thinketh in his heart about love; as he thinketh in his heart about God; as he thinketh in his heart about the devil; as he thinketh in his heart about the world; as he thinketh in his heart about his in-laws; as he thinketh in his heart about the church . . . whatever a man thinketh in his heart, that is what the man will project. You don't have to read somebody's mind; all you have to do is listen to them talk because most people are speaking out of an abundance of their heart.

How did this get into their heart? It got into their heart through the door of their mind. That is why there is such a battle for the mind. When a person gets saved, they become born again. What gets saved in them is their spirit. Man is a triune, or three-part, being. He is a spirit, he has a soul, and he lives in a body. When he becomes born again, that man gets his spirit born again; not his soul or body. John 3 teaches that we are born of the spirit and our spirit is recreated immediately. The Holy Spirit comes and lives within our spirit. As for our soul and our mind, that is in progress and in the process of being saved.

In James I, the Bible says that you are to receive the engrafted Word, which is able to save your soul. In Romans 12, it says, "Be not conformed to this world, but be ye transformed by the renewing of your mind." So, the mind and all of our thought processes and thinking patterns are not saved upon new birth. They are simply in the process of being saved. You determine how quickly that process takes place by your exposure to the written Word of God.

The body, of course, is not yet saved and Paul said, "I bring my body under subjection," meaning that I bring my five senses, that natural part of me under subjection. It is very important for you to see the body is the final thing to be saved; of course, in that day corruption will put on incorruption, weakness will put on strength, and mortality will put on immortality. The only thing really saved here is the spirit, meaning that your mind is open game. That is why the devil wants your mind. That is why the world wants your mind and even you want control of your mind. That's right, YOU. You also want control of your mind, but guess who else wants your mind . . . the Holy Ghost, the Lord Jesus Christ and the Heavenly Father.

Almighty God wants your mind so that He can first deprogram you and wash away and take away all of that stuff which shouldn't be there, and then He can reprogram you. He will begin to implement and input the memory which will cause you to be strong and vibrant and to project on the screen of life all of the good things, all of the powerful things and all of the positive things.

Remember, the Bible teaches this: there are only two schools of thought. There are only two kinds of wisdom: one is from above and one is from below.

When you feed on the wisdom that is from above, you will reap the reward and gain all of the attributes and the fruit of what that wisdom from above generates.

When you partake of the wisdom that is from below— the earthly, devilish, sensual wisdom—you will reap and show forth in your life those characteristics and those qualities. In the natural realm, it is eating; you are what you eat. In the spiritual realm or in Christianity, you are also what you eat. If you take in wisdom from above, you are going to be walking in the Spirit, flowing in the power of God, and reaping the reward of the Kingdom. If you walk in the wisdom that is from below, you are going to live earthbound and sensual. You will pick from the tree of the fruit of the flesh. You will be struggling, waffling, vacillating, in and out, up and down. There will be many things that will be your bedfellow. You won't be very happy in that place. Therefore, it is important that you crave and desire and put forth the effort to get the wisdom that is from above. As you see the wisdom from above and as you hear the wisdom from above, it goes onto that conveyor belt and it gets channeled into that brain of yours.

Your brain is simply the outside organ; the house for your mind. The brain is the organ that you see, and the mind is the part you can't see. The mind is something that is inside the brain. That is the part the Bible talks about needing to be renewed. <u>You need to renew that mind.</u>

The average brain weighs about three pounds and contains about twelve billion cells, each of which is connected to ten thousand other brain cells, totaling one hundred twenty trillion brain connections. It is no wonder that the brain has been called one of the most complex organs in the human body. It supervises just about everything you do from the involuntary beat of your heart to the conscious decisions of your life. It controls your hearing, your sight, your smell, your speech, your eating, your resting, your learning, your prejudices and everything else that makes you act and behave the way you do. Some things you inherited at birth. Your personal traits and even your growth are controlled by your brain and that mind of yours that lives inside the brain. It is absolutely incredible. What you see, what you hear and the way you think . . . these are the most significant influences in your life.

The chief function of the mind is the memory and the memory bank. There is the conscious state and the unconscious state. Everything you have ever seen, heard, touched or smelled is recorded in the lobes of your brain, never to be forgotten. Some of the information goes down into cold storage, or into the subconscious. Some of that information remains in the conscious state. This is why you are not immediately able to remember a lot of things you have experienced. You can't recall it, but you may be walking in the mall, walking downtown, or you may be on a trip and something will trigger a memory. It will be brought up out of cold storage. Everything you have ever seen or been a part of, everything you have experienced or learned from the time you were a baby until your current age; everything gets stored. Nothing gets away or gets lost. That's right. Nothing is lost. Even those who have some struggles in their memory later on in life and have been diagnosed with a particular disease, those memories are still there. They are still logged somewhere in the computer of their mind.

That is what the brain is usually compared to; a big computer that carries and stores a lot of memory which can be called up at the push of the button. So, it is an incredible process by which God made us. That is why He said that we are "fearfully and wonderfully made." He wasn't saying that we are all created perfectly, as perfect physical specimens. What He was saying is that we are so complex. The human anatomy is so intriguing. From its blood cells, to cells, to capillaries, to arteries, to veins, to the organs and the way they all work and function and feed and trade off with one another—it is absolutely Almighty God.

I want to tell you something more about that mind of yours. As your mind goes, so goes the rest of your body. As your mind goes (the mind and the brain), so goes your pituitary, your heart, your nervous system and your circulation. A healthy mind is probably the best nutrition and the best healing power one could possibly have. I am not talking about mind over matter. I am speaking about having the right kinds of thoughts, God-kind of thoughts, the Jesus-kind of thoughts to feed your mind and to give it strength. Then, as your mind generates all of those right thoughts, it feeds into the conveyor belt of the deepness of your subconscious and into the conscious state. All of the sudden, what you put in comes out. The old quasar "garbage in, garbage out" or "quality in and quality out" is reality. What you put in is what comes out. If you put in garbage, garbage comes out. If you put in precious treasure, precious treasure comes out. If you take the time to put in what is good and right and eternal, then what is good, what is right, and what is eternal will project.

Whatever you load onto the memory of a computer will come up at the push of a button. In many ways, our minds and the entire process is like one, big computer. Your mind needs to think on your recovery. Your mind needs to have something to hold onto in order to believe that it can be healed, that you can be better, that you can walk again, talk again, smell again, feel again, love again. The key word there is "again." Many have experienced the precious things of life: health, a loving relationship, a healthy feeling of self-worth, and a high value of their individual person, but for some reason, through the wear and tear of living, an attack of the devil or some personal wrong choices, some things just didn't go right. All of the sudden, they are down and they are bleeding. When you are down and bleeding, down and out, flat on your back with nowhere to go, it is there that your belief system will either make you or break you. If you haven't taken the time to store the right kinds of food into your mind . . . if that conveyor belt and everything you have been looking at, hearing and experiencing . . . if that conveyor belt has not fed the right kind of brain food into your mind and caused you to have muscle in the mind and to be strong . . . then whenever you are down and out, whenever your back is up against the wall, fear and panic and trauma is going to be your closest friend.

On the other hand, if you have taken the time (and it does take time) to get the God-kind of thoughts, the faith-filled thoughts and the Bible thoughts into your brain, then regardless of what you encounter (it may hurt, it may be something which delays the inevitable, it may be something that knocks you down), YOU WILL OVERCOME!

Solomon said that the word in your heart will bring health and flesh to your whole body. Therefore, it is very important that we do as David did in Psalm 119. He said, "Thy word have I hid in my heart . . ." What he was saying is I have swallowed that word. I have taken it in with my eyes and my ears. And even though I have made some bad choices, even though the devil has attacked me, even though my back is up against the wall, sooner or later that word will be in there working mightily and will come and rescue me from whatever has a hold on me. That is the power of the Word of God.

STRONGHOLDS

n I Corinthians 4, the Bible mentions strongholds. The great Apostle talked about strongholds that currently reside in the minds of men. That is right! That is where strongholds are. They are between your ears! It is a <u>way of thinking</u>. It is an ingrained thought pattern. It is either inherited or adopted, or it is learned. It can be either or all. It is something that has been there a long, long time. It has been formulating and is brought about and made strong as it is rehearsed.

Anything you rehearse becomes strong. Any muscle that you exercise becomes firm. Anything you practice, you become good at doing. A lot of us are very good at thinking wrong things. We are very good at thinking badly, especially when it comes to recovery from sickness, disease, dysfunction and personal problems that have been happening over the years. Our personalities, our way of dealing business, the dishonesty, the things that are hidden in the hearts of man, all these strongholds are the cause of many of our deep-seated emotional disturbances. Those memories that cause pain and friction in our everyday lives with our families, our children and our relationships at work . . . these are all strongholds. They just won't go away easily. You just can't say, "I won't think on that anymore." They have taken a long time to formulate throughout our lifetime, and they have to be dealt with efficiently and effectively or else they continue to set forth the policy of our lives.

That is happening to people today. They are living out the policy they inherited from their parents, the policy they adopted in their educational system, and the policy they learned along the way through friends, through relationships and through working opportunities. But strongholds are deadly, and they have to be pulled down. They have to be met head-to-head and toe-to-toe by the blood of Jesus and by the Word of God. Then, God can deprogram and begin to reprogram you, to get you thinking about recovery, healing, strength and success the way God wants you to.

These strongholds are formed by several things. I want to list five of them for you:

1. **Parental Strongholds:** Probably the most common way strongholds develop in the mind of a person is through their parents. During the formative years, from the womb of the mother until the children leave home, they are on the front row seat. They watch mom and dad handle problems. They watch mom and dad handle pain, sickness, trouble and just general disturbances throughout life. Things are being calculated on the lobes of their brain, in their minds, as they watch how mom and dad interact when faced with chicken pox, cancer, accidents, tragedy, and the bills.

Even at an early age, children calculate things. Are mom and dad always running to the doctor? Are they fearful? Are they hiding things and not telling it all? Are they relying on homemade remedies? Are they always yelling and cursing and swearing? Do they throw things around the house?

On the other hand, do these children see their parents praying, reading the scriptures, going to church and reaching out for prayer? When it comes to recovery, it rains on the just and the unjust. If they live long enough, most people will have the experience (and I am not saying it is a good one) of handling their fair share of heart pain, body pain, mind pain and confusion. The challenges are waiting for all of us. That is why the Bible says we have to work out our own salvation with fear and trembling.

It is very important that children, in their formative years, see mom and dad properly handling problems in their lives. Is it always a different brand of medicine? Do they go from Tylenol to Bufferin to Anacin?

Are they a walking drug store? Not that medicine is bad, but are they constantly relying on it as their source? Do they always go to the movies to eradicate personal pain by getting lost in some movie plot? Usually that movie plot is from someone who is ungodly, has no values, and sometimes is an enemy of the cross of Christ. Yet we will pay $12.00 or $15.00 to walk into a movie and give our minds over to a Hollywood producer and let him line the shelves of our mind with all kinds of evil, violence and filthy standards. Do our children see that? Do they see us getting our own way because of temper tantrums? Or, do they see us listening to praise music and good preaching which is available on the television, radio and internet? It is available in every city, every town, every nook and cranny of society. This world is being flooded by the Gospel of Jesus Christ, because Jesus said it shall be preached to the whole world; then shall the end come.

At an early age, children watch how their parents pursue recovery. Do they get discouraged quickly? Do they get their spirits broken? Usually, what a parent portrays to a child is what that child develops as a thought pattern, 'that is what dad did, that is what mom did," and they will carry out some of those same patterns. This is inherited. This is one of the ways in which a stronghold, or a way of thinking, is inherited. Mom did this in this way and dad did it that way. These strongholds usually last for a lifetime.

2. **Religious Strongholds:** How you see God at an early age
will determine how you receive help from God. So many people
are raised in a religion that is impersonal and had nothing more
to do with God than to show up at some service and listen to a
man speak about God. The underlying feeling is one of "you
have to be good enough, and you have to earn it. You always
have to be doing something." The grace message is very shallow.
The messages of the power and the promises of God are often
lost in the places that have stained-glass windows, a steeple and a
bell. What happens is that most people don't get an opportunity
to hear from a Holy Heaven, but they hear from soulish man.
They hear a man's ways, a man's belief, and this becomes their
belief. How you see God will determine your spirituality. If you
see God as someone who is angry with you; if you see God as
someone far away from you; if you see God as someone who
just wants you to read and recite and sing; if you see God as
someone who just wants your tithe, your money, your property
or your land; if you see God as someone who just wants you to
take a day out of your week so you can feel better about yourself.
. . if that is the kind of religion you are brought up in, then in the
time of trouble you are not going to sense and feel a personal
Jesus next to you, caring about you. Jesus is trying to get the
anointing and the power of His love into your life to keep you
and restore you regardless of what happens.

The Bible says that neither height nor depth nor power
nor principality above, in and under the Earth can separate you
from the love of God. God loves you! He wants you to know it,
to feel it, and to experience it. He wants His love to keep you.
That is why the book of Jude says to keep yourself in the love of
God. God has a keeping power. He is not a religion; He is a
person. If your perception of God is a religion or nothing more
than a building where you go and sing out of the hymnal, if He is
nothing more than "Somebody way up there in the sky," then
loneliness and fear will govern and direct your thoughts for
much of your lifetime. Many religions teach that you cannot get

near God. Many religions teach that you have to do this or that in order to please God. You have to pray so many times a day, chant or do so many works. The Bible does not teach that. The Bible teaches that He is the high priest who is touched by the feelings of our infirmities. God cares. He said, cast all your care on me because I care for you.
(I Peter 5:7)

Religion plays a big role in how you see yourself getting healed, getting into recovery and, ultimately, how you relate to God. How you see God is how God will be able to help you in the time of trouble.

3. **Teachers and Education:** The third way strongholds develop in our mind is through our teachers and our educational system. From an early age, there are so many things that we begin to learn from our teachers. So many of them are seemingly harmless. I think back as a young boy and some of the nursery rhymes that we listened to such as Jack and Jill who went up a hill to get some water. This is a poem about tragedy. Jack falls down and here comes Jill. That means that what happens to others is going to happen to you.

There is Little Miss Muffet who sat on a tuffet. Here comes a spider, and she is afraid. She has fear inbred in her about animals and creeping, crawling things. This is just the opposite of what the Bible teaches.

There was an old woman who lived in a shoe and had so many kids she didn't know what to do. She was an old woman. She lived in a big old shoe called poverty, where she was destined to have nothing, to see nothing and to live hard the rest of her life.

There was Humpty Dumpty who sat on a wall and had a great fall. Nobody, not even the King's men or the King's horses, could put him back together. That means that some things were terminal, irreparable and irretrievable. They cannot be fixed.

All of these are just the opposite of what the Bible teaches and what God promises. Those things are seemingly innocent, yet they get into us at an early age and begin their deadly purpose. Remember what I say: everything that gets into your mind stays in. It affects us until it is <u>deprogrammed</u> and <u>reprogrammed.</u> Until that time, it is like a bad tape that has bad things on it. Until you tape over it, that tape is playing and in some way is working against you.

There is teaching on evolution, where man wasn't created but rather he came from the ancestor of apes or from some biological ooze that crept up onto the seashore and evolved into a higher form of life.

There are alternative life styles that are presently being taught in our universities and in some schools. Homosexuality is taught as an alternative lifestyle; that it is something you are born with and it is okay to violate yourself in this way.

There are many ways to get help today, but God never wants you to get help anywhere except through Him, because if you compromise and get help through another so-called belief system where Jesus is not the center, you are allowing yourself to receive at the expense of compromising your convictions and your standards with your own God. You can never compromise your standards with your own God. I am telling you that this literature out there has to do with drugs, treatment, therapy, rehabilitation, evaluation, analyzing, and on and on. There are so many processes out there that are borderline and need to be looked at very, very carefully. Our entire education system is right now in a position to condition the minds of men at an early age. They want to formulate their belief system about evolution, about homosexuality, about how to recover from problems and pain, and about who to turn to. Throughout our lives, our teachers and our education system are part and parcel of what we feel and how we believe; even how we approach getting recovery!

4. **Personal Experiences:** It is very difficult to get past this because you, personally, have experienced it. So many people formulate what they believe and stand for all of their lives because of what they have experienced. One of the toughest strongholds to get away from is personal experience.

People will buy a certain car. Then, if they don't have success with that car, they actually begin to say, "I will never own that type car ever, ever again." They begin to transmit that to all the people around them. You see, they had a bad experience with that car. Someone else may have had a good experience with it, but they had a bad experience, so in their minds, never again.

They may go to a restaurant and get some meat that wasn't properly cooked, or maybe they got some eggs that weren't properly cooked. They may have gotten a drink that wasn't properly prepared; it wasn't hot enough or cold enough. They may have had a bad experience so in their mind, they will transmit, "I went to that restaurant, don't go there. They have bad meat, bad eggs and cold coffee!" It may be that one experience which formulates this stronghold. It may be the fault of the cook in the kitchen and not the restaurant, but in their minds, it was a bad experience. That bad experience begins to equate into "don't go there!" This is especially true if you go on vacation somewhere and the hotel wasn't all that it was cracked up to be. Neither was the beach, and neither was anything else there that was projected on the brochure, so in your mind you will say, "Uh-uh, I am not going back there. That was lousy food, bad sun, the beach wasn't nice and the water wasn't warm. It just wasn't anything it was cracked up to be." In your mind, you are never going there again. So, it is important that you see that personal experiences you have with life and with people often result in you developing a strong opinion about a certain matter.

Getting past our own personal experiences is something we all need to be open to. Just because it happened once doesn't

19

mean it will happen again. It is like when Peter went fishing and didn't catch any fish all night. He worked really hard. Then Jesus turned around and said to him, in Luke 5... come on, let's go fishing.

Peter said, "But we have toiled all night and caught nothing." Peter is saying, "I have had a bad experience, and I know that there is nothing out there." He couldn't get past his own experience. Once he allowed Jesus to take him past his own experience, he began to see that there was something there to catch. It is very important to see that strongholds often come out of our own poor, bad or negative experiences which we then allow to dictate policy in our lives for a long, long time.

5. **The Hollywood Ride:** This is simply a combination of the movie and music industry. I wrap them all into that one and call it "the Hollywood ride." Our lives are influenced and our personal beliefs and preferences (the way we dress, the way we act, the way we believe, our philosophy in life) are made by the Hollywood movies to which we have been exposed. Movies dictate what marriages seemingly should be. Movies dictate the way a man should act, the way a woman should behave, and the way children should respond. The movie industry is directly responsible for many deviant behavior patterns, especially when someone is watching a movie and then, either consciously or unconsciously, begins to believe or act in a way that is uncharacteristic of what the Bible would want them to. No one else knows, because it is often in the privacy of one's own home or one's own mind, but God knows. He sees where you are getting your policy. He sees what is influencing you. It is not Matthew, Mark, Luke, or John. It is the movie industry...Warner Brothers, Metro Goldwyn Mayer—Hollywood. It is the rock star, the movie star, the athlete, the whole syndrome of personalities out there. That is who is affecting your policy . . . not the good Word of God. As that goes, so you go.

When the Beatles arrived in America back in the 60's, they revolutionized the world. Guess what, just before them it was Elvis Presley. Before him, there was someone else, and the beat goes on. Today it is a different name, a different guitarist, a different drummer, or a different song. It may be someone who is in country music, someone in rock music, someone in pop music, someone in classical music, or someone into the rap scene. The Bible says, "Let everything that hath breath praise the Lord." The Bible also says that all the glory goes to God!

We see that Hollywood (in its movies and its music, in its pool of celebrity icons, athletes, rock stars and public figures who are no more living for God behind the scenes than some of the most evil people you have read about) has a way which is influencing, directing and setting forth a policy for living that is absolutely frightening. So many of the people who have committed serial crimes against women, who have raped women and small children, later were discovered to have been an advocate of pornography or the movie industry. So, it is either there graphically or it is there subliminally.

Today it is not okay to watch a movie where they disrobe, but it is okay to watch a movie where they advocate adultery, where they advocate the stealing of money to make something right. It is amazing how we strain at a gnat and swallow a camel. We say "no" to what is obvious but "yes" to what is obscure. That is the deadliest thing of all; drinking a subtle poison which has no odor. It is like carbon monoxide, odorless but deadly. It gets into the system of the mind and the brain, and you begin to think in a way that is so wrong because Hollywood says that most things are solved in one hour.

In any program you watch on television where people are shot, most good guys never die. It is only the criminal, the bad guy, that dies. However, in the real world it is not like that. Most things are not solved in one hour. Most things don't work themselves out between 9:00 and 10:00 p.m.

It is important for you to see that most of the songs which are sung are sung out of somebody's painful experiences.

Let me tell you something, as they go, so I do <u>not go</u>. I don't have to go where they went. I can go somewhere different and somewhere better. I don't have to cry into my drink. I don't have to say she left me last night and went down the road. I don't have to listen to those songs, "This is the dawning of the Age of Aquarius." This is not my dawning of my Age of Aquarius. This is very important. You may sing the song, "No Where Man." Well, I am not a "no where man." You may sing, "I am a loser." But, I am not a loser! I was born to win! I was destined to fly with the eagles, and that is the way God wants to see you.

So, we see these five important forces that are out there . . . your parents, religion, the education system and the teachers of a child, your personal experiences, and "the Hollywood ride" of celebrities, movies and the music industry. Imagine all five of these embodied into one mind. It is not like each individual in life picks out one of these and is influenced by it. Today, most are influenced by all five of these throughout their lives. Just imagine the strength of all these: the strength of the parents' influence, the strength of religion, the strength of personal experiences, the strength of what your teachers have taught you, and the strength of what Hollywood has injected into your system. Think of all of that working in you, and here you are. You are in a position where you need to be healed. You are hurt. Things haven't worked out. You reach down inside to find something that will help you, and look what you are drawing from . . . a library of stuff, of information which didn't work for your parents, of a religion which hasn't answered anybody for anything in a long, long time; a personal experience that is "iffy" at best; a Hollywood lifestyle which isn't real; what you see on the screen is a lie. You begin to reach down inside yourself for help and find that you have been building your life on sinking sand; not on the Rock.

Strongholds . . . they are strong and they have a hold, but guess what? When there is anything strong that has a hold, there is something stronger that has a better hold. There is the stronghold of JESUS CHRIST! He is ALL power! He is ALL strength! He can break that cycle of madness and sickness in your mind. He can deprogram and reprogram, he can brain wash and control and set forth a new policy that will bring healing, health and restoration to your whole life!

STARVING YOUR MIND

Strongholds capture your mind and hold you hostage. Your feelings, your thoughts and your body continue to carry out the orders these strongholds have stored up for a long time. You want to feel better. You want to be healed. You want to move toward a normal and personal recovery, but your mind has become a garbage dump of negative, pessimistic, wish-washy, mediocre thought patterns. There is no muscle on the mind to fend off these voices of deadly discouragement, and you don't know where to turn or how to get help. Is it too late for you to start?

In Romans 6, Paul speaks about yielding your members. It is a powerful chapter. What he set forth in that chapter in that the one to whom you yield your members to, is the one to whom you will be a servant and a slave. If, however, you yield your members to life and to righteousness, you will be a servant and a slave to LIFE and to POWER. If you yield your members to things which are of the flesh and carnal; you will be a slave and a servant to that very force. It is "who" you yield your members to that determines the outcome.

What are your members? Your members are your eyes, your ears, your mouth and your thoughts. If you yield those members, this means that you have a choice in the matter. That is what I want to you hear. You have a choice! If you are reading

25

this book right now and you find yourself up against the wall, surrounded by enemies, with that sinking kind of feeling that you are about to quit, about to throw-in-the-towel, I want you to know right now that you don't have to. THERE IS A WAY OUT! It is very important that you grab hold of that.

One way out is that you begin to starve the stronghold. You begin to starve that way of thinking. That simply means that you must begin to take charge and monitor everything coming into your mind. In II Corinthians, the Bible says that it is important that you bring every thought captive into the obedience of God. In other words, every thought needs to be arrested. Any good business has surveillance, a monitoring system of who is in their parking lot and who is driving in and around their building. This makes a bold statement that they value the contents of their building or their property.

You need to value the contents of your mind. You need to value the contents of what God wants to get into you to make you a better person, a stronger person, a more fit and proper person in order to live a highly successful life for the Lord Jesus Christ, as God intended! Sometimes, you have to do things and make decisions that are uncomfortable and unpopular, at least for a season, until you can get back on your feet. You have to take charge of your own life. You have to, because if you don't, who will? If you don't affirm yourself, then who can affirm you? You first have to get on your own side so other people can get on your side with you. If you are against yourself, then you are a kingdom divided against itself. One of the things you have to do is to begin to say "no" to some people around you, who may be very dear to you, but their input at this time is not the kind of input that you need to hear. They are feeding your stronghold; they are not pulling it down. They are not accelerating progress; they are holding back progress. They are good people, and you love them. They could be your family. They could be some very dear friends around you and, for a season, even though you may miss them, you need to fill that time slot with Jesus. Excuse yourself and choose to be with the church, with the Word of

God, and hang out where the anointing is. You must pull away from that mudslide of negativity; the mudslide of bad reports, the mudslide of "things are impossible." Begin to starve out that thought pattern. Don't let it be fed anymore by friends and family. Explain it to them; you don't need to tell them they are bad. You don't need to tell them you can't tolerate what they are saying. You need to tell them that right now you need some personal time, some solitude, some time alone with God. You need to think some things through and allow God to begin to get some muscle on your mind so you can fight off what they may be saying. Just because mom and dad says it doesn't make it true. Just because friends say it doesn't make it true. Just because it is fact, doesn't make it true. Facts change. The truth never changes. So, it is important that you see that there has to be some kind of monitoring system for these thoughts which come in; for some of the things we have been fed; for some of the things that have come down the assembly line—through our eyes and ears, from our moms and dads; which have not been accurate and need to be dealt with, so God can begin to honor and bless the true and faithful witness. He blesses and honors the truth, and He needs you to do the same.

It is important that you see and understand this "starving" process. You may have to begin to starve yourself from the way that your pastor or priest is teaching and preaching. The main things you are listening to from the Word of God and from mass or from church, ask yourself, "Does it work for me? Is it producing fruit? Is it forceful? Is it impacting? Is it changing?" Not: Does it make me feel good, but is it making me change? Is it bringing health and recovery, or is it bringing condemnation? Is it helping me to be free from prison, or is it locking me up? Am I feeling better about myself or worse about myself?

There may come a time when you need to take a break from the church you attend or from the preacher to whom you are listening, especially if you are sensing that what is being told to you isn't helping you but is actually making the problem more complex. Not every man in the pulpit is preaching the truth. Not every man on television or on radio or writing a book is teaching you the right way. Believe it or not, some people are in it for the money. Some people are in it for position. Jesus said that some people are just hirelings and don't know the truth or have the truth in them. They are deceived. They are the blind leading the blind, so you need to find out now if the person to whom you are listening and the church where you are attending really care about you and the rest of the people. If they are reaching out to you, if they are wanting to touch you, wanting to be a hands-on Good Samaritan pouring in the oil and the wine, by all means continue. If, however, you are sensing that you are being judged, condemned, and scrutinized, and you are not being fed and prayed for and counseled, you may possibly need to pull back and starve out something that may be feeding that stronghold in a way in which you are not aware.

You may have to starve yourself from watching television. That is such a hard thing to say. It is easier to say than to do, but that is something you must begin to do because what is coming through that television, for the most part, is corrupted except for Christian programming and some other possible wholesome films. Everything is downward, wisdom from below, and it will only feed your problem; it won't bring any kind of healing or health. It may touch your soul but it will not bring any kind of healing or restoration. It may stir up some feelings, but you don't want <u>feelings</u> stirred up; you want <u>healing</u> stirred up. Did you get that? You don't want feelings stirred up; you want healing stirred up. You may have to say right now, "I am going to put myself in television quarantine. I am going to close my ears to secular music. I am going to close my ears to rock, to country, to pop, and to classical."

In Psalm 32, David said surround yourself with songs of deliverance. He didn't say to surround yourself with childhood, youthful, easy listening or light music. He said to surround yourself with songs of deliverance, songs that talk about the blood, songs that talk about the cross, songs that talk about the stripes that Jesus bore, songs that talk about the power of God, songs that talk about the things that Jesus preached and taught and said and did. Those kinds of songs you want to be going over and over in your mind. Paul said it best in Ephesians 5, "Speaking to one another in songs and hymns and spiritual songs, singing and making melody in your heart to the Lord." That is what God wants you to be rehearsing in the deep recesses of your mind, and that is what will help you accelerate, catapult and skyrocket with speed back into the realm of recovery, healing and power, in the name of Jesus.

Initially, you may have to starve yourself from parents, from family, from friends, from some of your own church friends, from your leader and from outside literature. You have to put down those magazines, as innocent as they may seem. They don't have to contain pornography, murder or violence. They just have to contain things that aren't producing healing and power.

If you have time to pick up a sports magazine, you have time to pick up the Bible. If you have time to pick up a fashion magazine, you have time to pick up the Bible. If you have time to pick up a magazine about better homes and better gardens, you have time to pick up the Word of God. It is important that you see that there is a book which brings health to your flesh. Many books will just keep you where you are and fill your mind with a false hope; ever gaining knowledge but never coming to the truth.

So parents, family, friends, possibly church, possibly your pastor, possibly church people . . . all need to be considered while in personal recovery. There are a lot of places you need to stay away from because they don't produce an environment that is conducive to your recovery. You don't need to be where you see people half-dressed. You don't need to be sitting and eating where you hear rock music pounding over the airways. You don't need to be where alcohol is being served. Whatever the case may be, you may have to starve yourself from some places for a while. I am not saying to starve yourself forever. Do it until

29

you get back in charge; until your mind recovers; until you are able to get rid of some of the bad and put in some of the good; so that your resistance is built up in order for you to submit to God and resist the devil and he will flee. Then, you should be able to walk everywhere you want with your full armor of God and accomplish the high purposes of Jesus.

While you are in the process of recovery, you are susceptible to everything and every person that possibly carries a transferring of spirits . . . that is when evil spirits jump from one person to another. You have to break out. You have to stay away.

In Psalm 23, David said, "He leadeth me beside the still waters and restoreth my soul." What was David saying? God took him out of the mainstream. He took him out of the city and into the country; away from people, away from his environment, into a place where he could be so absorbed and locked in—to a place where he could do a quiet and strong work of restoration in his mind and in his heart.

Sometimes God will remove you from your familiar environment so the influx of wrong can be stopped. He may not have to take you far away, but just for a while you need to break some of the predictable patterns which you have developed over the years . . . who you are with, what you listen to, what you laugh at and the jokes you agree with. All of that can be raw sewage coming into your mind; causing you to not move toward a healthier mind, a healthier body, a healthier personality or a healthier life.

Understand something. What you feed is what will become strong. That is what Paul meant in Romans 6 when he said; "To whomever you yield . . ." What you feed is what you yield to. What you feed will get stronger.

If you put two dogs in your backyard, feed one and starve the other, the strong dog eventually will beat up on the weak dog because the weak dog has no strength. It is like anything else. You put two plants in your window, feed one with water and starve the other. One plant will grow and the other plant will wither. This is called the law of life. What you feed gets strong. What you feed gets nourished. So, whatever you are feeding your mind will control you. If it is wrong places, wrong people and wrong things, it will have a withering kind of effect and your stronghold will continue to dictate the policies for your life. But, whenever you begin to starve the flesh and feed the spirit with the right people, the right places and the right things, your spirit is salvaged. You can hang out with the right people— not perfect but right—and you can go to right places. Those are places where Jesus would go and walk, and sit and fellowship, and have a good time. Whenever you begin to absorb right books, right television, right music and you begin to challenge the very thresholds that have been with you a long, long time. You may cause a few people to get upset.

Your mom and dad may say, "Why are you doing or not doing this anymore, not going there anymore? We didn't raise you that way."

They didn't raise you correctly in every way. Thank God for the right they do, but there is a place where your parents cannot be God. Your church cannot be God. Your friends cannot be God. Your experiences cannot be God. There is a place where Hollywood cannot be God. It doesn't matter what they say or what they think. It only matters what Almighty God thinks. It is He who went to the cross for you; not them. It is He who shed His blood for you; not them. It is He who deemed it necessary to come back from the dead, not them. Thank God He did!

It is important to see that there is a price to pay when you begin to starve one and feed the other. When you starve a little and feed a little, your strongholds will fall a little and gain a little. Some may try to do both. They will starve a little, feed a little; starve a little, feed a little. That is the kind of results they will get. When you look at the whole scenario of how you do it, your approach to starving out these things will determine how long those strongholds stay with you. How long you procrastinate will determine how long you put off the recovery you can have.

You can begin recovery today that will accelerate you into a better place and a new place before you can even think about it. Or, you can wait and be here a year, five or ten years from now. You will begin to experience muscle on your mind, and your "refuter", that part of your mind that inspects every thought, will say "No way! No thanks!" Whenever someone gives you their opinion about a policy or procedure that is contrary to the Word of God, you will begin to say, "No thanks" and pull it down because you now have <u>muscle on your mind.</u>

FATAL THINKING
PART 1

In today's society, there is a fatalistic feeling that is looming everywhere. People are under the impression and under the strong persuasion that there are not too many safe harbors in their lives. What they eat, where they live, what they drive, what they buy, where they go . . . there is a fear lurking over the land today like never, ever before.

They say the average person in New York City has two chains, a bolt and a bar on their door; four locks for every door. There is a feeling of danger and insecurity in the inner cities today. An unfortunate reality of our society proves that one of the most dangerous places to live is in the womb of a mother. Meaning that if you are the baby in the womb, you have a statistically high percentage of never making it into the known world.

Then, there is the drunken driver. How many people today are out on the highways at the mercy of somebody coming down the road inebriated on some alcoholic or drug substance?

We also have the ever-present threat of terrorism everywhere you go. There are plastic explosives being found from the Olympics, to the plane, to the mall, to McDonalds. There is terrorism worldwide. You have movies such as "Fatal Attraction" where you don't know who you may be looking at who may later stalk you. It may be a man after a woman; it may be a woman after a woman. There are no social barriers anymore. So we have fatal attractions, the HIV virus and then there is Ebola, the flesh-eating virus which is sweeping the country. Do you get it by contact, do you get it by fluid, do you get it by touch? No one really knows.

There is a rising flood of teenage suicides and young people who are taking their lives because of seemingly no purpose or hope for the future. All of these constitute a fatalistic world. They are all deadly, they are all true, and they are all statistics. But let me tell you something that is more fatal than all of these combined. It is the way a person thinks inside their mind about how God sees them, about what God wants to do for them, about the plans that God has for them. In Jeremiah 29:11, it says that God's plans are for good and not for evil; that He has something for you to be. He has something for you to do. He has something for you that will cause the potential of your life to come forth with such power and explosion. He wants to bring healing into your mind. He wants to bring healing into your body. He wants to bring healing into your heart. He wants to bring healing into your life so that you will be "every wit whole."

God's plan for you is wholeness; nothing less. He didn't just heal one leper; He <u>healed</u> nine lepers, but only one leper was made <u>whole</u>. That's right, one leper was made whole; the other nine just received a <u>physical</u> healing of the disease. But the one man was healed on the inside of his soul. He was healed in his mind, his emotions, his heart and his body. That is what God has for you. So, what is the road block? What is the hindering spirit? What is the force that is fighting you and keeping you from moving forward?

In this chapter, I want to deal with the most common, fatalistic thought patterns which are prevalent among Christians today and which keep them from grasping all that God has for them.

Fatalistic Thought Pattern No.1: *God is angry with me
and is against me.* People have a perception of God as someone
waiting for them to make a mistake. When they do, they will be
severely punished. So many people have never been taught the
grace and the loving side of Almighty God. They were
indoctrinated at an early age that God is governed by do's and
don'ts and governed by a lot of Old Testament law and legalistic
thinking . . . an eye for an eye and a tooth for a tooth. If you
make a mistake, the stone comes at you, the hammer falls, and
you are punished. There is nowhere in the Bible where God says
He punishes the righteous. He chastises the righteous, but He
punishes the wicked. There is a difference between chastising
and punishing. God never punishes the righteous. God, with a
loving hand, chastises like any normal parent would, because if
you spare the rod, you spoil the child. The Bible says you show
more love by correcting. In that way, you are saying that you
want to break a lot of the generational curse and negative
patterns which are forming in a young child. The Bible says that
foolishness is in the heart of a child but the rod of correction
will drive it out. In no way is God angry and in no way is God
waiting for an opportunity to discipline you, take privileges away
from you or restrict your lifestyle. Many come into this world
and are indoctrinated into that side of God. They never see the
loving side of God; where God thinks about you day and night,
where you are the apple of His eye, where you are the treasure of
His fields. He says that it is the Father's good pleasure to give
you the whole Kingdom. God wants to bless you above and
beyond whatever you can ask or think. "Eye hath not seen nor
hath ear heard the things that God has in store for you." So God
is not an angry God; He is a loving God. He can be provoked to
anger, but I believe more than God getting angry at the
Christian, He gets hurt and grieved because He sees the
Christian living far below the privileges and the level of life that
is available to them.

Some people perceive God to be like their earthly father. They relate to their Heavenly Father as they do their earthly father. Maybe all they ever knew in the earthly relationship with their physical, biological dad is that form of anger and an abusive nature, possibly even to the point of physical abuse, sexual abuse and/or mental abuse.

There are all kinds of cruelty in today's world as far as father and children. So often, a person carries that relationship over into the Kingdom when they get born again. They begin to relate to God like that, because that is all they know. God is not like that. He is not against you. In Romans, the Bible says the opposite, "If God be for you, who dares to be against you." God said that nothing would separate you from His love: not height, not depth, nor power, nor principalities, nor things in this world or the world to come will separate you from the love of God, for we are more than conquerors in Christ Jesus. We have to deal with the thought pattern that God is angry with me; therefore, I am being punished for something I have done wrong. That is why my back hurts. That is why my eyes are bad. That is why my kidneys are failing. That is why I have been allowed to be addicted to drugs or alcohol. Not at all! Not at all! God loves you and he is planning right now for your recovery and your restoration. He just needs for you to allow the Holy Spirit to break this fatal thought pattern and allow it to be destroyed. The Bible says that it is the anointing that breaks the yoke. That means that it destroys it, never again to be put back together.

Fatalistic Thought Pattern No. 2: *I can do it in my own strength*. I have come through many tough times, and I can do it my own way. One of the worst things a person, including a Christian, can think is that they can accomplish or achieve anything apart from the help of the Holy Spirit. There is a verse in the book of Zechariah that says, "Not by might, nor by power, but by My Spirit, says the Lord."

One of the greatest things you can learn is that there are many things that are much bigger than you. Oftentimes, it takes some hardship and the school of the Holy Spirit to find this out first-hand. Because of the indoctrination of the thinking which says, "if you want it, go for it; whatever you think, you can have; whatever you want to do, you can do it; if you work hard, put your time into it and sacrifice, etc., etc." A lot of this sounds good, but what a lot of it is saying is that you are really your own God. Whatever you order, you can have. It is true that there are a lot of things you can accomplish on your own, but that is where the hardship and the frustration comes in, because a lot of things you have created are man-made, self-made, and willpower will only take you so far. That is the general thought. "I can do it. I can make it . . . I . . . I . . . I." Pretty soon you begin to think you can conquer anything. You get your heart broken and think, "I can lick this; I will beat it." So often, what is secretly working behind the scenes on your behalf is the mercy and the love of God. He goes before you and clears the path; hoping you will recognize His righteous and heavy hand in your life, making a way for you. All too often, not only do we fail to recognize it, we take the credit for it. That is when deception comes, and we begin to think, "I can do it." Guess what happens? Inevitably, God will let you come up against something you can't beat. He doesn't like that. It is not God's heart to do that, but He needs to do that because He wants you to turn to Him out of your own volition, your own free will, so that this fatalistic thought pattern of "I can make it, I can do it" can be broken. There is a verse in the Bible that we all know, Philippians 4:13, "I can do all things through Christ," but the latter part of that verse says "through Christ, which strengthens me." Sometimes we forget the last half of that verse. It doesn't say "I can do all things." It doesn't say "I can do all things with a little Jesus." It says, "I can do all things," because of, in and through the person of Jesus Christ. Does that mean that you can swim underwater for one hour without an oxygen tank? Of course not! Can you swim underwater for one hour with an oxygen tank? Of course! That is the extent to which you can do anything with or without Jesus. Can you do anything without Jesus? Some things—yes; most things that are of value and of powerful substance—no! You need the power of Almighty God working in you.

We must pull down and break that fatalistic thought pattern. You are dependent on Jesus for your next breath, your next heartbeat. You are dependent on Jesus Christ for everything and all things, and that is the only thing that can pull down and break apart that fatalistic thought.

Fatalistic Thought Pattern No. 3: *Whatever is supposed to be will be.* If I am supposed to be a millionaire, I will be. If I am supposed to live, I will live. If the marriage is supposed to stay together, it will stay together. You throw your life, your health, and your future into the hands of fate, F-A-T-E. Not faith, fate. What you are saying is that whatever is supposed to be will be. That is a lie! That is so fatalistic. What it does is remove any personal responsibility on your part to press in, to pray, to read your Bible, to call on God, to get spiritual advice, to sit under the anointing, to run to the Rock that is higher than you. The name of the Lord is a high tower; the righteous run into it and they are not afraid. They are safe. It takes away and avoids personal responsibility of running to God, of being diligent and seeking the scriptures to see what God has for you. It takes away any kind of contribution on your own part. What it says is, "I am just going to do whatever I am doing, and whatever is supposed to be will be." That kind of thinking opens the door for the devil and his demons to come in and begin to work havoc in your life. If you leave your life in the hands of circumstances, you will be swallowed by one fish, then the next fish, then the next, and so on. You won't live from glory to glory; you will live from crisis to crisis.

God wants to change the circumstances effecting your natural world. He doesn't want you to sit back and say, "God, do it." God wants you to come to Him. He wants you to seek Him early in the morning. Call on His name and He shall save you.

He wants you to seek and search for Him with all of your heart, and then you shall find Him. He is looking for you to put on the full armor of God. He is looking for you to go to the upper room and know the Holy Ghost. He is looking for you to be touched by the prophet, the apostle, the pastor, the teacher and the evangelist. He is looking for you to show forth the effort that causes Him to release all that He has for you and to begin to change your health circumstance, your job circumstance, your family circumstance and your church circumstance. Circumstances are not the truth. They are fact, but they can be changed. Goliath was a circumstance, but he went away. The fish that swallowed Jonah was a circumstance, but it went away. So, circumstances, as seemingly difficult and as big as they are, can be changed. They won't automatically change, but they can be changed as you become obedient and move into what God wants you to do. You throw the rock, and He will cause your giant to fall.

Fatalistic Thought Pattern No.4: *I am different.* So many people hear the great stories of victory encountered because of the help of Jesus, because of the help of the Word of God, because they went to a healing service and got healed, because they received counseling over the phone and were helped. So many people listen to stories of victory and breakthrough over the television, on the radio or receive them in the mail, and they sit back and say, "Well I am so happy those people got help, I am so happy she got healed. I am so happy their marriage was spared. I am so happy that someone mysteriously gave him some money. I am so glad for them, but you just don't understand. My situation is different." All too often, the person in the crisis somehow chooses to believe that what God can do for other people and what has happened for other people is nothing less than a divine intervention. Yet somehow, when it comes to their own struggles, they vacillate, they struggle, they waffle and they waiver. They say, "But I am different." Let me say, of course, you are different. Everyone is different. There are no two snowflakes alike. Our DNA is different, our fingerprints are different, our relationship with God is different, and yes, we are not all looked at as the same by Almighty God. He made each of us uniquely different. We are compared to a net full of fish that are all different. That is the way God sees us, but He loves us all the same. He is no respecter of persons in that He loves us and wants us to draw from the benefits of the cross. So you are different to Him in name, in purpose, in body shape, in gender (male or female) and where you were born. As far as what He has for you (the benefits), the Bible was written by Holy men of old and inspired by a Holy Ghost moving over them, what God has done for one, He will do for another. He wants to heal you. He wants to bless you. He wants to prosper you. That is something that is straight across the board. In that regard, you are not different. You too can go to the Fountain that never runs dry. You too can touch the stripes on His back and be healed. You too can find the coin in the fish's mouth and be blessed abundantly. You too, as you tithe and give offerings, can have the windows of heaven open up unto you, so you are not different in that aspect. You are no worse off than anybody else. It may seem so because you are in this situation. When you are in it, it is the worst to you, but I want to tell you something. God has the power, God has the willingness, and God has the way to bring you out of wherever you are and to take you wherever He wants you to be. Therefore, you have to stop the fatalistic thought pattern that says, "I am different."

The Bible says that Elijah was a man of like passion. That means that Elijah, as mighty as he was, as strong as he was, still had that little bit of fear of man in him. This caused him to renege of the mission he was on and to hide in a cave until God worked with him a little. He was a man of like passion, which means that we have the same Savior, we have the same enemy, and we have some of the same problems. So, you are not so very different.

If you could see the human race as God does, there are many like you who are struggling with what you are struggling with; in pain on the inside, troubled in their minds, problems in the family, finances shaking and quaking. There are many situations, so you are not so very different. Just because God has not brought somebody across your path who is similar to you doesn't mean that you are alone. It doesn't mean you are isolated and are some kind of weird case that is the only one on planet Earth. God has saved you especially for Him, to bring healing and His power into you. He wants to do something so great it will cause your life to have new meaning and a purpose that will shake and shock all who know you; because your story will be an incredible story of the restoration power of Almighty God.

FATAL THINKING
PART 2

<u>atalistic Thought Pattern No. 5:</u> *I am still paying for the sins of my past.* There are many people in the church today who love the Lord Jesus Christ, who have already been forgiven of their sins, but who live in such a house of guilt. Everything that currently goes wrong is somehow connected to a dot in their past or something so horrific and bad that they did.

Let me tell you something about that. That is a lie, an absolute lie from the very pit of hell. It is an onslaught of the devil attacking the mind of a precious saint of God who has been weakened and not yet come into the acceptance of his or her forgiveness in Christ Jesus.

In Isaiah 1:17-18, the Bible says, "Though your sin be as red as crimson . . ." What is the prophet saying? Though they be dark and deep and stained (that is what that color meant), when you reason with God, He will wash you and make you whiter than white. There is a power of God that, once it touches the deepest and darkest spot in your life, doesn't just get covered like the Old Testament blood of animals; it goes away. It is purged and removed like the New Testament blood of Jesus. That is what you have to believe, and that is what you have to accept. That is what you have to fight to bring about in your daily life. It is time to quit paying for the sins of your past. Move on. Either the blood of Jesus works; or it doesn't work. If it doesn't work, we are all in trouble, but if it does work, walk in it.

I don't know about you, but I don't like to keep paying for something for which I have already paid. When my car is paid off at the bank and they mail me my title, I don't keep sending them money just for the fun of it. I need that money, so I just say, "Hey, this is paid for."

When I purchase a suit at the store and bring it home, it is paid for. I don't send money to the department store and say, "Hmmm, I like that guy so much I am going to keep paying for my suit." No! When you have paid for something, it is "Paid in Full." You don't continue to pay.

That is the way it is with your sins. When you are forgiven of whatever you have done and have received forgiveness, you don't keep paying for your sin. One of the ways you keep paying for it is by relating what is going on in your life right now to something you did in the past. You may still need some healing. You may still need some deliverance. You may still need some extended counseling, but let me tell you about the "forgiveness" part of it. You are forgiven! You now qualify to stand in the Holy of Holies. You now qualify to stand and grab the promises of God. You now qualify to walk in deep, intimate fellowship with the Lord Jesus Christ, the Heavenly Father, and the Holy Spirit too. So, you must break out of that fatalistic thought pattern where you are still paying for something you did one year ago or ten years ago; perhaps in some cases, thirty and forty years ago, and in other cases, a lifetime ago. You say, "But what if I did something that was so bad?" Well, there are many people in the Bible who did many bad things, and sometimes we fail to see that God's grace came to them anyhow, and they were forgiven.

Abraham almost turned his wife over to a heathen king, but God forgave him. David took a man's wife and killed the man, and God forgave David. There was Rabbi Saul, who was killing Christians, and God forgave him and changed his name to Paul. There are so many people who did so many wrong things.

Peter denied the Lord three times at the fire, and Jesus loved him back into the place of fellowship. Those men didn't go through their lives looking back and saying, "Oh, I made a big mistake. I committed a crime." No! They moved on into the place of apostleship, into being pillars of the church and writers of the Gospel. You too need to break that fatalistic thought pattern which thinks you are still paying for the sins of your past. We are used to believing that way because, in man's world, you never finish paying. You never serve enough time. Once you are in the dog house in man's world, you are in the dog house forever. Once a leper: always a leper. Once a loser: always a loser. Once a junkie: always a junkie. Once a prostitute: always a prostitute. Once a wife abuser: always a wife abuser.

When you come to the cross where the blood flows freely and runs deeply and where there is an endless supply, you can be free! Once a prostitute, now a holy woman! Once an abuser, now a lover! It changes because the blood is what changes you. It converts you from the inside to the outside, and that is what breaks you free from the law of sin and death in your mind. You need to break the power of the fatalistic thought that you are still paying for something in your past. That is not true!

Fatalistic Thought Pattern No. 6: *It is too late.* Have you ever heard that it was too late? We are baptized in and engulfed into thinking everything has an expiration date. In our society, we are nurtured that everything has an expiration date on it. Once you pass the expiration date, from your credit card to your insurance policy, you move into penalty. This is only good for a certain time period. The sale ends on this date. When they are having a great sale, all of the department stores have a specific date for when the sale will end. This offer is only good until such a time. Bread and dairy products such as milk have an expiration date stamped on them. Beyond that date, the product may not hold its value. Everything has an expiration date on it, and that expiration date says that once you don't do what you

are supposed to do by that time, it is no good. It is too late. It is
over.

Then there is the realm of physicians and the doctor's
report or the marriage counselor's report . . . too little too late;
too much, too late. That kind of thinking often gets engrossed in
your mind and you then put a death sentence on your health, on
your marriage, on whatever you are currently fighting for in your
life. You begin to believe it is too late. It is over. My feelings are
gone. My faith is gone. The disease is too widespread. My
diagnosis is no longer imaginable to be overcome or defeated. I
have been worn down. I came into Christianity too late. I got
hold of the faith message too late. I am just not versed on what I
should do. It is just too late for me. I am too old. There are
many who feel they are too old to be healed, but in our healing
services, I see people in their 70's, 80's, and 90's who get healed
of deafness, blindness, osteoarthritis and osteoporosis.

God is never, never of the thinking that it is too late. As
a matter of fact, if you look in the scriptures, you will see that
Jesus seemed to favor or cater to a lot of people who had long-
standing problems, long-term illnesses. Somehow, He moved
toward them; not away from them. The man in John 5 was
crippled for 38 years. That is a long time. That is 38 birthdays
and 38 Christmas'. He couldn't walk. He lived and dwelt among
a pool of infirmity as people sat around that pool hoping and
believing to get in the moving water. Yet, after 38 years of being
paralyzed, Jesus came and touched him and set him free.

We have the woman who had the issue of blood for
many, many years, yet she pressed through and got her healing.

You have the woman who had the back that was
hunched over. She had been like that for 18 years. Jesus came
and said, "Be loosed from thine infirmity." In Mark 9, there was
the epileptic boy who had terrible demonic bondage since he
had been in his mother's womb. Jesus came and said, "Come out
of him, thou unclean spirit."

On and on, there are people in the scriptures who
seemed to have had illnesses (physical, mental, emotional and

spiritual) for years and years, and yet Jesus came and with one touch, one spoken word, He changed everything. I believe the reason, Jesus favored many of these people with long-standing problems, was to demonstrate that it is never, I repeat never, never, never, never too late!

We have to get out of thinking that we are beyond the expiration point. It may be the midnight hour or it may be in the fourth watch, as it was when they were on the sea, the storm came and Jesus came to them. Why he waited until four in the morning, I don't know, but he came. Why didn't he come when the water was not yet in the boat? I don't know, but he came. The idea is that he came.

Why did Jesus not come before Lazarus died? I don't know, but he came. Did it seem too late in the eyes of man? Yes! Was it too late for God? No! It is never, never too late! God is always on time! Whatever you are believing and standing and fighting for, it is important that you see it is not too late. It is not too late to know. It is not too late to be healed. It is not too late to start over. It is not too late to be strong and it is not too late to dream. It is not too late. You can begin now by reaching out and trusting him at His word and trusting that everything he has for you, he still wants to bring about in your life. "He, who began a good work in you, shall be faithful to complete it until the day of Christ Jesus." (Philippians 1:6) We must break down and destroy that fatalistic thought, "It is too late."

Fatalistic Thought Pattern No 7: *The grasshopper complex.* "I am so insignificant. I am so ashamed of my life. I haven't accomplished anything. Who am I? That is the same thing Moses said to God. Many do not feel worthy for God to visit them and move in them. They have never received the right amount of recognition, the right amount of credit, the right amount of confidence from mother and father or surrounding groups to input into them the awesomeness and power they can have in the name of Jesus. Therefore, what we have today are many who have bought into the lie of the standards of the world. They base a lot of their value and their worth on what they look like. Today, it is very important for you to look a certain way in your physical anatomy. To look a certain way is in, and to look another way is out.

Personality means so much today . . . how you smile, how you walk, how you communicate. In some circles, it is important where you work and how you carry yourself, but it has no determining value as far as your personal value to God and what He wants to do in your life.

Status means so much today . . . your position, your title. Oh, my, he is a doctor. She is a lawyer. He is Vice President. He is CEO. He is an entrepreneur. All of the sudden, what this does, in very subtle ways, is convince people they have not done anything, they have not achieved anything, they don't have any productivity in their lives; therefore, why would God want to help them? God wants to help more important people than them.

We also have those who seem to think God doesn't want to help anybody who has made mistakes or has fallen and done things which are less than wonderful. They have made many business mistakes and family mistakes, and they have blotches on their record. They have a criminal record. They have done thus and so, and God doesn't want to do something in their life because they are not spotless. God wants to do something in your life because He is spotless. Some people think God blesses according to their behavior. Obedience does bring a certain reward, but God's system isn't, "If you behave, I will heal you." God's system is, "I am going to heal you and that will help you to behave." God's mercy goes forth beforehand and touches us in different and powerful ways. It is the goodness of God, the Bible says in Romans 3, which causes us to want to be different and to change everything from our morals to our mind. That is something which has to be dealt with because God does not want to move in your life with the cattle on a thousand hills; God does not want to move on your life with the wind in the upper room; God does not want to move in your life with the seven thousand, seven hundred promises of His word because you behave. He wants to overwhelm you with His goodness! He wants to shower you with His blessings! After He does this and you realize He did it, not because of how good you are, but because of how good and great He is, it breaks your heart and causes you to look up and say, "What a mighty God we serve!" Hallelujah!

We need to break down this fatalistic thought pattern of being ashamed, of not being worthy, of being like a grasshopper in the eyes of our enemy.

These fatalistic thought patterns, all seven of them, are the most common that have come across the particular ministry in which I am involved. It breaks my heart to see people bound, ball and chain, to these fatalistic thought patterns.

I want to say that these thought patterns can be broken. The trees can be cut down and the stumps can be pulled out. The ground can be plowed and ready for fertile soil. It may not happen overnight, but the journey of one thousand miles begins with the very first step. I am telling you, God wants you this moment to be set free from the chains, oppressions and the yoke of bondage, never again to be entangled.

I believe even as you read this material that he is challenging some of the negative, pessimistic, deadly, toxic thought patterns which have been running and playing in your mind like an endless movie. A never ending tape. God is saying, "I am going to rip out the tapes. I am going to destroy the software. I am going to deprogram you, and then I am going to reprogram you to stand in the high places of the Earth and to be healed by my power, to be healthy once again, to think once again, to feel love and to love once again, because I have set my everlasting love upon you!

ADDICTED TO THE WORD

These fatalistic thought patterns have to be dealt with aggressively. They have to be confronted and challenged head-on. There can be no time-out, no vacillating, wishy-washy, half-baked, room temperature approach to something so deadly, so toxic, so focused on stopping you and causing you to be ravished by pain, anguish and frustration all your Christian life. NOW is the time to face it; to step forward and march toward that fatal giant that has been stalking you, plaguing you and mocking you most of your life. Hear my cry, in times of crisis, many run to the altar for prayer and many step into a counseling room and say, "Pastor, counselor, would you talk to me?"

In the time of crisis, you will swallow a pill or take a shot. But victory is not in getting help in the time of crisis, because most people, out of a knee-jerk condition, get help only long enough to fend off immediate danger. They get help long enough to temporarily delay that which is trying to destroy them. They get some kind of minimal, nominal help. Then, one or two weeks later, perhaps a month later, they are back in the same crisis.

There has to be something stronger; something bigger and better; something more potent that what has hold of them. The answer has to be more than a quick prayer, a quick touch, a little bit of oil on the head or some soft advice. There has to be a high commitment to the uncompromising Word of God. The Word of God has to become the key foundation that begins to wash your brain, or "brainwash" you. We use the term "brainwashing" so much in a negative sense, but in actuality, all of our minds need a good cleansing, a good brainwashing, a mind washing.

In Ephesians 6, the Bible says we are washed by the water of the Word. There is a literal brainwashing that goes on when God's word begins to pierce and penetrate your mind. It gets down into the cradle of these strongholds, the cradle of this fatalistic thinking, and it stops the merry-go-round. I mean it casts the merry-go-round back into the deep, dark sea. Something new begins to happen. God can then begin to conform you. God can then begin to transform you and renew your mind.

How does God renew your mind? How does He transform you from the inside? He does it by the Word of God; by the renewing of your mind by the Word of the living God. That Word of God has to become the most important, prioritized literature that you read and take into your mind, more than any other piece of literature on the planet.

Today, many are so engulfed with so many books. Today, everybody is reading something. Our bookstores are filled not just with wrong information but with fiction, novels, magazines, and newspapers. People spend more time on a crossword puzzle than they do in the only Book of Life. I am telling you, right now it is time that we begin to put forth a conscious effort and a high commitment into the book that enables you to have what you are reading. Today people are reading books about better homes and better gardens, but they don't have a better home or a better garden! Today, people are reading books about muscles, but they still don't have any muscles! Today, people are reading books about fashion and clothing but their closets are still running empty!

You may not have what you are reading about in those books, but in the good Word of God, it is settled in the heavens He watches over His word to perform it! You can have everything and all things that you read in that book! But, you must be committed. I am not talking about being committed in the sense of some days "yes" and some days "no." I am not talking about being committed when you feel like it. I am not talking about being committed whenever it is an emergency and the Bible becomes your "911." I am talking about being committed to the Word of God the way a drug addict is committed to drugs. I am talking about being committed to the Word of God the way an alcoholic is committed to his booze. I am talking about being committed to the Word of God like someone wanting to commit suicide. That is why we use that phrase, "he committed suicide." He was committed to taking his own life.

We understand commitment in a negative sense. It sometimes takes a negative connotation to help you understand the significance of a word or of a happening. That can be so much more powerful and beneficial to you in the spiritual realm. That is, a commitment to the book that Jesus left behind; a book that will revolutionize you, change you and cause you to be happy in who you are, in what he has called you to do, and who he has called you to be. It will cause you to be the head and not the tail, to trample on serpents and scorpions and over all the power of the enemy. This book is anointed! This book is inspired! This book will cause you to have an unction from on high—from the Holy One. But, you can't snack on it. You can't take in television, radio, magazines and, of course, the negative press along with all of the other news broadcasts of the media circuit. You can't have your faith by staring into a computer while surfing the internet and gaining so much information. None of that is able to rescue you in the day of trouble, but this book, known as the Word, is not of man. This book is not known as the word of angels; this book is not known as the word of scientists or philosophers. **THIS BOOK IS THE WORD OF GOD.**

How can we approach the Word of God? I want to give you some easy steps on how you can begin to break down this book from Genesis to Revelation and get it inside you. You are about to swallow the most lethal pill of inspiration you have ever had in your life. It is time to overdose on the Word of the Lord. It is time to shoot-up the name of Jesus into your spirit and that will cause a high that you have never, ever had before. I am not just talking about trying to get you out of the crisis you are in. I am talking about getting you walking down a path where the snake bites, but it can't hurt you anymore. Just shake it off and throw it into the fire. I am talking about submitting to God, resisting the devil, and he will flee from you.

Principal No. 1: *Hear the Word.* You have to allow yourself to be subjected to the Word of God and committed on a regular basis to hearing it. You have to hear the Word of God. Romans 10:17 says, "Faith comes by hearing and hearing by the Word of God." You have to hear the Word. Whenever you hear the Word, you are allowing yourself to receive the truth into your ears, which goes into your mind. You are allowing yourself to be confronted with the truth. You are allowing issues in your life and other fatalistic thought patterns to hear what God says about some of the things you are thinking. God has to be true, and every man a liar.

You can't let God be true if you can't hear what God is saying. Sometimes you can't hear God for hearing man. Often, the messenger who is trying to get the truth to you is a turn-off. You don't like him. There is a clash or something so that they are not appropriately attractive to you. That is why the book is in written form. It is not dependent or contingent upon a personality. Whether it is a woman, a man, a married couple, a church or a denomination, it is written in black and it is written in red. It is down in print, and you can't hide or run from it. It just <u>says</u> it, and that is what you have to deal with, but you have to <u>hear</u> it.

There is a voice. How do you hear the Word of God by reading it? Because when you read it, you begin to hear it. When you read you begin to see it. When you read it, it talks to you, and that word (faith comes by hearing) as you become subjected to that book, it is like anything else. The more time you spend with anything, the more you get to be one with it. The more you understand it and know it, the more it will begin to talk to you. Faith comes by hearing and hearing by the Word. When you begin to hear the Word, you can't hear what you want to hear. You can't hear for somebody else. Many hear for other people. You can't hear for some day. You have to hear for NOW. You have to hear for you. You have to hear for today.

Sometimes, you may have to force-feed yourself. When you are in the hospital, too tired to eat or too sick to eat, they stick something in your arm called an intravenous needle and they force-feed you. Your body needs the vitamins and minerals shot into you because you are too tired, too weak and too sick to eat, so something has to be done. Your body is force-fed by intravenous means. Sometimes you have to force-feed your soul and spirit, because you are not in the mood. You are upset. You are angry. You are too tired or too weak. What has to happen is, that you have to turn on the television, you have to put in the video, you have to get the audio tape, and you have to sit back and allow yourself to receive.

How do you do that? You HEAR. You begin to hear. You let your ears begin to become trained ears. Often, we bend our ear to trouble, and we bend our ear to crisis, to death, disease and destruction. It is time we bend our ear to the Word of God. Because in that book, He tells you about living long, about being happy, about being prosperous, about being strong, about your family being saved and going to heaven. In that book, He talks to you about all good and great things, but you have to <u>hear</u> it. Are you ready to hear and, as you hear, are you ready to listen?

Principal No 2: *Meditate on the Word.* Commit yourself to meditate on the powerful Word of God which will change the harmful mindsets that create fatalistic thinking. Meditation is when you begin to look at something and think on that same thing over and over and over again. It means to mutter, to turn it over in your mind, over and over and over again. It is like when a cow chews down its cud spits it back up and eats it again. It is something that is repetitive. It is dwelling on something. It is something you do over and over again. You dwell on it and think on it.

Joshua 1:8 says, meditate day and night on the Word, and you shall prosper and be successful. Meditate day and night. There are a lot of things you will read and see which you won't remember. If you don't remember it, what good is it? There are a lot of things you will see at face value, and you will not understand what good it is. There are a lot of things you will see at face value and you will not be able to put into your life because of it being so foreign to you. So, what do you do? There is only one thing to do. Like anything else, you must spend some time with it in order for it to become real to you, so you can take from it that which it is offering you. Many things in the scripture are so foreign to the way you have been thinking because the way you have been thinking is wrong. It has taken you a long time to get to where you are. You have spent a lifetime thinking about yourself the way you do, thinking about God the way you do, and thinking about life the way you do. This is why they are called strongholds. They have a strong hold on your mind. They have your mind held hostage, and they don't want your mind to come into anything new, especially anything new that is true. All new things aren't true, but some new things can be true, especially if they are grounded in God's Word. If it is new and true in God's Word, then the stronghold is through. Do you hear me? If it is new and true, strongholds are through! Fatal thinking has to pack its bags and get out of your head because God has His thoughts on the way from heaven, through

His Word. You have to take the time to begin to read it, hear it, and dwell on it.

If you have a disease, if you have a sickness, that bad report is real to you. How does that mind go from natural to carnal to spiritual? Your mind is transformed as you meditate on the Word of God and His promises for you. You must face that natural man, that carnal man, that bad report, with the promises of God found in his Word. As you meditate on it and think about it, you know it is not the sudden splash that breaks a rock. It is that constant dripping, that constant drop, the consistency of something over and over and over again. This will cause it to become real to you. If you are thinking on God's Word on a regular basis, you can't think on wrong and right at the same time. The moment you begin to dwell on the truth, you can't dwell on the negative. You can't listen to that spirit of fear, that voice of fear that is talking to you, that voice of lust that is talking to you, that voice of the bad report that is talking to you . . . you can't think on two voices at the same time.

If you are thinking on the Word of God, it has an anointing around it. It is powerful and sharper that any two-edged sword, dividing even the thoughts and intents of the heart. It divides the soul and the spirit, the joints and the marrow of the bone. (Hebrews 4:12) It is a sword. When you meditate on the Word of God, you are letting a sword pierce and do spiritual surgery on your mind. It begins to cut out negativity and cut out all of this stuff that is wrong. Meditating, dwelling, thinking, over and over and over again, on what God has said which is contrary to what your circumstances say, is contrary to what your natural or carnal mind says. It is contrary to what the doctor says. It is contrary to any outside force, demons and devils, and any other voice. Sometimes, you can't actually get to know what you are reading right away because it is so different from all of those other voices.

What do you do? The only thing you can do is begin to dwell on it, repeat it, pray it, and turn it over and over again in your mind. What happens is that it sinks from your head down into your heart. You no longer just <u>believe</u> what you are reading; you <u>know</u> what you are reading. What the meditation power has done is cause something to become bone of your bone and flesh of your flesh. God's Word will now begin to move in you. Remember, before Jesus SPOKE the Word, He WAS the Word. Before you speak the Word, it is good for that word to be a part of you. The way it becomes a part of you is because you have meditated on it and now you know it. Hallelujah to the Lord!

Principal No. 3: *Speak the Word of God.* The first principal was for you to hear the Word. The second principal was to meditate on the Word, and the third principal is to have a high commitment to begin to speak the Word of God.

I understand that many people don't know what to say. Well, it has already been written for you. The script has been written, and it is holy. Hallelujah! It is called the Holy Scriptures. It is a script that has been written by God himself. Jesus used it when He was here. If it worked for Jesus, it will work for you. The devil doesn't have to always act or react by what you say, but in Jeremiah 1:12, it says "I watch over my Word to perform it."This means that the devil, sickness, disease, and curses, all that stuff out there, responds and backs off at the spoken Word of God.

It is the spoken Word that created the world and the universe. It is the spoken Word that Jesus used to heal the sick and cast out devils; the spoken Word—not just the Word, but the SPOKEN Word. That is what the sword of the spirit is, in Ephesians 6. The sword is not just a Bible laying on a coffee table somewhere. The sword of the Spirit is whenever the Word comes up out of your spirit and out of your mouth and off your tongue and goes forth to accomplish that which it is purposed to do. It doesn't return void. It falls in line with what Solomon said, "The power of life and death is in the tongue." Your tongue releases heaven or hell, life or death, blessing or cursing. It is not something you make up. It is not just positive confession. This is word confession.

Positive confession is whenever you are positive for the sake of being positive. "It won't rain tomorrow. It is going to be a better day ahead. Things are going to get better." That is general and positive, but the Word of the Lord is chapter and verse.

"As your days, so shall your strength be." (Deuteronomy 33:25)

"I can do all things through Christ who strengths me." (Philippians 4:13)

"My God shall supply all your need according to His riches in glory by Christ Jesus." (Philippians 4:19)

"But as for me and my household, we will serve the Lord." (Joshua 24:15)

"Believe on the Lord Jesus Christ, and thou shalt be saved and thy house." (Acts 16:31)

Speaking the Word is releasing the power of the Word. It is what Jesus did whenever he was in the wilderness and the devil came after him, tempting him all those times. In Matthew 4, each and every time, Jesus would respond by saying, "It is written . . . it is written . . . it is written." He was speaking the Word, and the devil backed down each and every time. It says that the devil lost that battle, and Jesus came out of the wilderness in the power and demonstration of the Holy Ghost. It is important that you speak the Word.

So many of us have grown up in the kingdom, in the church, and we have learned how to say, "in the name of Jesus, in the name of Jesus." We know how to say, "I plead the blood, I plead the blood." "I rebuke you Satan." Those are all fine. Every single one of them is fine, but we have to be careful because we can hide behind that and never have to force ourselves or press ourselves to learn the Word. We hide behind these little one-liners, but you never want to take lightly the name of Jesus. You never want to take lightly pleading His blood. You never want to take lightly rebuking the devil. God is going to hold you accountable for your growth and what you know in Him. He wants you to learn the Word. He wants you not just to say little phrases and rely on them your entire life. Can you read? Can you study? Are you putting time into the newspaper? Are you putting time into other literature? Are you putting time into reading this and that? If you can read and you are spending time reading other things, God wants you to convert and begin to get into His Word, to get it into you and into your heart, to discipline yourself to begin to speak it. Then, out of your mouth won't come cursing, out of your mouth won't come negative flow, and out of your mouth won't come a double-blinded man. Out of your mouth will come the power of the spoken Word.

Jesus said, "Whosoever shall say unto that mountain, be thou removed and be cast into the sea and shall not doubt in his heart, he shall have whatever he saith."(Mark 11:23-24) Therefore, we see that hearing the Word, meditating on the Word and speaking the Word is a powerful principle which begins to break down, little by little, the strongholds, those fatalistic thought patterns that have inhabited your mind for so long.

Principal No. 4: *Mix the Word with Faith.* This means you are to put action to the Word, put legs to the Word. You are hearing it, you are thinking on it, you are speaking it; now ACT on it. It doesn't say if you feel like it. It doesn't say if you think you are ready. It says to act on it NOW. Receive it NOW.

In the book of Hebrews, it says, "And mix the Word with faith." What does that mean? It means that a lot of times we have read the Bible for so long, and we believe, but we can never act on it. You can believe something all you want, but if you don't act on it, you will never benefit from it or glean the reward of it.

You can believe water is wet, but until you get in it, until you act on that knowledge, you will never know it. You can believe that ice cream tastes good. I believe it, but unless you act on it, you will never know that ice cream is cold and tastes good. You have to act on it or enforce it. You can believe that if you turn keys on the car, the motor will start. You believe it will, but unless you act on it, you will never know that it will.

Acting on something is so powerful because it takes you out of the realm of wishful thinking. It removes you from dreaming and fantasizing, and it moves you into an action. That is when God can begin to bless your next step. Whenever Jesus told the lepers to go and show themselves to the priests, they acted on His Word. It doesn't say they felt like it. It doesn't say they wanted to. A lot of things in life you will not want to do, and you won't feel like doing, but if you will just act on what the Word says, you will still receive the reward from it.

When the Bible tells you to give ten percent of your money to God and bring it into your church, into the storehouse, so that you may have meat and drink . . . a lot of times when you look at what you have, you don't feel like giving up a tenth. Yet somehow you say "I know it is true. I know it is true," but you don't feel like doing it. If you will just act on it— just do it—you will be like the man that built his house on the rock because he is a doer of the Word.

If you just hear it and believe it but you never act on it, you are like the man who built his house on the sand, who is a hearer of the Word only. If you are always sitting in church saying, "Amen, I believe it! Hallelujah! That's right! Preach it, brother. I agree," and you walk out of the church and don't act on what you hear, you are like a man who builds his house on the sand. If you don't act on it and give a tenth, if you don't act on it and forgive, if you don't act on it and pray, if you don't act on it and speak to your mountain, then you are like a man who builds his house on the sand. The storms come to both, but what Jesus said is that when the storm comes to the man who is building on the rock, his house isn't shattered and ripped to pieces. It is left standing tall and strong.

The man who builds on the sand; the man who sits in church and says, "Amen, I believe it! Hallelujah! That's right! Preach it, brother!" and doesn't act on it, the storm will wipe away his house. He will find himself always rebuilding, always trying to recapture what he once had, never able to go forward because he is too busy repairing what he had. He can't seem to manage because he is not acting on what he believes. He cannot live life on good intentions. People say, "I intended to do this. I intended to do that. I intended to do the other." God doesn't bless your good intentions; God blesses your actions. Faith without works is dead, like the body without the Spirit is dead. That is what the Bible says in James. So, unless there is a course of action that is taken and followed by that which you are saying and that which you are professing and believing, it is lifeless.

If you begin to believe that you are healed and that Bible verse says this and thus, then you are beginning to act on it. When someone asks you how you are doing, you can say, "I am healed by the Word of God. It possibly hasn't manifested in my body yet, but by His Word I am healed. I am calling those things which be not as though they were. (Romans 4:17) I am speaking to my body. I am believing that the Word is for my body. It is going to bring health to all of my flesh. I believe now, in my heart and in my mind, that I have the money I need. It may not be in my hand, but it is in my mind and in my heart. I believe it now because the Word says it. My family is saved, even though they don't look saved, smell saved and act saved, but in the faith realm, I believe it because the Word says it!"

When you begin to act on the Word, it builds your faith. It causes you to begin to see your circumstances in another way. It causes you to see your family in another way. It causes you to see everything in another way because now you are acting on the Word of God. As you hear the Word, as you meditate on the Word, as you speak the Word, and as you act on the Word, mixing it with your faith, it begins to break up thought patterns. It is like WD40 on a rusty bolt. It begins to loosen the crud and the grime of what is holding that screw in place, and it causes it to be smooth so that it flies right out of its socket.

Whenever you begin to constantly come against all the fatal thoughts in your mind with the Word of God, by doing it, by acting on it, you begin to break up the grime and the slime that has had a hold on you for so long. All of a sudden, you find yourself being set free from the oppression of the devil which is in your mind. This is the way that fatal thinking patterns are destroyed, obliterated and broken into tiny pieces.

The power of God is real. This is how you get long-term health. As I said at the altar . . . quickly! In the counseling room . . . quickly! With the anointing of oil . . . quickly! In a crusade . . . quickly!

You have to change the long-term thinking patterns that are in your mind. That comes by slowly turning things around. It is not like turning a rowboat; it is like turning a big ship, which turns gradually until it gets to the place where it begins to head back the other way.

That is what God wants to do with your mind by using this sharp, two-edged sword. It is sharper than any other two-edged sword; sharper than an philosophy book; sharper than any psychology book; sharper than any book known to man in any library; sharper than any other holy book in the world, and there are many. This is the one that is left standing tall and strong. This is the one that is forever settled in heaven. This is the one that is the more sure word of prophecy. This is the one that He exalted above His own name...THE WRITTEN WORD OF GOD.

SHUTTING DOWN THE WRONG VOICES TO KEEP THE BLESSING

There are volumes of voices that war against your mind to plant seed of fear and doubt, all for the purpose of stealing the blessing that the Holy Spirit has begun to work in you. These voices come out of your soul; they come from people controlled by natural knowledge, opinions, and education outside the pages of the only supernatural book on the planet. Sometimes these voices are right out of the pit of hell.

In II Corinthians 13:1, it says, "This is the third time I am coming to you. In the mouth of two or three witnesses shall everything be established." Everything be made a covenant, shall everything be written in blood.

Everything is established or finalized when two or three witnesses come into agreement. Agreement becomes covenant and a covenant is recorded in heaven, which enables the hand of God to be turned loose or tied up. The Word of God says it takes two. It is not like a jury where it takes five or you have a hung jury. God is looking for something to be established by two or three witnesses.

Whichever voice you come into agreement with will speak loudest in your head and capture your imagination

A lot of times you get prayer and the pain is better but it doesn't go away. Sometimes you get prayer for cancer and the tumor shrinks, but there are still microscopic cells. Sometimes when there is surgery for cancer, they take out all they can see, but there are microscopic cells, so you wait to see how the body reacts. Most doctors want to hit you with chemo. When someone is coming out of clinical depression or going through divorce, the road to recovery seems endless, with many setbacks. No matter how many times they get touched and there is progress, many have enough left over for them to take home and be responsible for. They are better, there is progress, and the man or woman who was ministering was able to break the strongman and allow the healing to begin.

After ministry of prayer, people still have symptoms. God allowed their problem to become reduced so that it is manageable. Now, you are the same size that your problem is. God took your problem and tied one of its hands behind its back to make the thing equal for you to fight, but God will always have you fighting in your fight. God will not have someone taking everything that is wrong out of your life. He will have you learning how to live by faith, fight with your faith, and watch God prove His Words to be true in your life. This is a beautiful way to harness and channel all of your aggression which you are now channeling in the wrong ways. There are a lot of unresolved areas in some of your hearts. You still have some pain, some anger and some hurt. You still want to vent all of your frustrations. There is no better place to channel your anger or to vent some of that aggression and some of the stuff you have in you than to begin not to settle for a teaching, not settle for being touched at the altar, but to take any residue, anything left over which is still causing pain and heartache and go home and see if his Book works for you. But how do you do that?

Paul says that everything is written in blood when it is established by two or three witnesses. Here are the three witnesses we are dealing with: I am one, God's Word is one, and whatever my problem is, is one. The Word has a witness, I have a witness, and my problem has a witness.

If you have a bad back, your back is talking to you and saying, "I have a witness; I need a healing."

If you have cancer, that cancer is talking to you and saying, "You have cancer and you need thus and so."

If your marriage is in trouble, it is talking to you. Goliath had a witness: "Come out here and fight!"

Your circumstance is talking to you. They wait for every waking moment of your life. They love reminding you of how much you don't have. They can't wait until you get up off the floor after you have been under the anointing, and they say, "I am still here!" They can't wait until you get home and they say, "Hi, I have been waiting for you. Was it a good service?" The next morning, you call the church and say, "Pastor, last night all that pain left. I went home and I was fine. Then this morning, every pain in my body came back." Your problem has a witness, and it realizes that by talking to you, it plays with your psyche. It plays with your mind. Sometimes your problem is encouraged because there are demons that jump in and say, "Yeah that is right! Things aren't any better." Sometimes these demons are encouraged because there are people around you like Job's friends. They don't understand what it is to be healed by faith. To be healed by faith has nothing to do with your feelings. Your pain may still be there, but according to you and your faith, you are healed by the Word. You have people around who think their job is to keep you in your integrity and keep you out of self deception. They will say to you, "Well, is the pain gone?" You say, "Well, I am healed according to the Word." It does not say that I got healed according to my feelings. I don't want to agree with my feelings because my feelings lie about half the time. I want to agree with what is true. I am a witness, the Lord is a witness. That makes two. Write it in blood. It is a done deal. The moment I agree with my feelings, I write in blood that I am not healed.

You have people all around you who want to ask, "Is the pain gone? I see your face, and it is still there. You didn't get it, but you will get it."

They are well intended, but you will say, "No, I am healed by the Word." Your friends will say, "You can talk to me. It's me." They are trying to pull you out of your faith, trying to pull you out of your confession. In their minds, they are trying to keep you honest, but there is nothing more honest than what God wrote. They don't realize that, but the faith realm is more real than any other realm. Until that realm becomes real to you, you won't be able to pull anything out of it.

You would not go to the grocery store if there was no food in it. You look through the window and you see food; that is how you know there is food in there. You have to realize that there is a Kingdom and in it are shelves filled with blessing.

It is like the story of the four lepers (2 Kings 7:8). God took them in and the tables were already set. You have to see the Kingdom as a huge department store with healings on this side, money on that side and blessings on another side. You have to see that you are going to get it.

There are people all around you and they get you agreeing with them "The pain is still there, isn't it? Well, if the pain is there, I know this faith stuff, this positive confession, but if the pain is still there, it means you are not healed yet."

It doesn't say that by His stripes you are getting healed. It says that by His stripes you were healed. Never come into agreement with those voices. Never take them lightly. They are on a mission of madness. Hearing something is one thing- but listening to it is another. Guaranteed, you will have to stand up in the face of people that you love and respect and make a stand that is contrary to their understanding. It may be your mother or your teacher, even your priest or pastor. When your faith walks in and your mind is set on the breakthrough blessing, you do not consider another voice. Romans 4:19 says of Abraham "….and not being weak in faith, he did not consider his own body.." Way too much consideration is given to outside voices and it creates a mixture that takes the power from the Word of God and from the end result that you so desire.

You have all these witnesses around your circumstances …the circumstance itself, the demons that use the circumstance and talk to you (you aren't ever going to get that; you aren't ever going to get this), and you have your own feelings. Can you ever trust your feelings? It depends on how close you walk to God. If you are Enoch, trust your feelings!! There is a great chance that what you are feeling is what God is feeling. If you are not spending that much time in the Word, in prayer and communion, laying before God and emptying yourself and letting God fill you, then your feelings can't be trusted that much. Why, because that is you. Your soul isn't saved yet. Your soul is being saved. You had better be careful when those feelings start to lead you down the rabbit trail. Is that what the prophetic word you received told you? Then you had better get back to that prophetic word and hold on to it. Is that what the written Word told you? You had better get back to the written Word. You had better not let feelings go with your feet. You better get back and anchor to that prophetic word.

You need to be writing those prophetic words down because those prophetic words are coming to pass. Praise God, they are coming to pass! When God gave you those prophetic words, He knew you were going to stumble and fall and sin and yell and swear and take snuff and smoke. He didn't give you a prophetic word and then say, "Let's have a board meeting. I didn't know he was going to smoke, I didn't know he was going to swear."

When he called Peter the Rock, He called him that long before Peter ever denied Him. He knew Peter was going to fail. Some of you have tripped and stumbled and gotten bloody knees since you have gotten a great word..guess what? That word is from God and it is coming to pass! You need to begin

69

agreeing with it and stop agreeing with your sin. Stop agreeing with your feelings. Get back and hold on to that word that somebody gave you or you gave yourself and you wrote it down.

If God said it, it will come to pass in its rightful time. I can't waiver. I can't go by my feelings. I can't let devils tell me. I can't let doctor's report to me. I can't let my mom and dad, my preacher, or my church break my agreement with the Word of God. God told Noah to build a boat, and there was not a cloud in the sky.

There may be something that nobody understands about my marriage, about my business or about my children. I may be holding on to a promise that seems will never come to pass. I can't afford to have friends like Job's to guide me and steer me. I can't afford to have a mom and dad come against me. I can't afford to have a church, brothers, sisters, and leadership come against me. I am going to have to stand. I am going to have to cast my vote. I am going to have to give my witness, not to them and not to those and not to this. I am going to give my witness to the Word of God, because He said it, He gave it to me, and I am going to sign it in blood.

You need to rehearse that to yourself and confess it to other people. Some of you need to get your friends together, especially the ones you're with the most, and set the pace for them so they have a rule system. Tell them, "By the way you know about my marriage. We have been hanging out and drinking coffee, and I haven't really been speaking faith to it. I go to a church and get prayer, and I come to you and bellyache. I tell you what I am going to do. I can't be a kingdom divided. I am not going to talk to you anymore in a negative way about my marriage. I want you to know I still love you, and I am still having some troubles, but by faith my marriage is already healed."

Failure likes to hang out with failure where they tell sad stories and share sorrow together. By doing that, they create a false comfort and really believe they are helping each other. God does not bring people together to swap sad stories without emphasizing His desire to intervene and somehow, someway bring glory and honor to His name. That glory is reflected sometimes in the change of our circumstances and sometimes in the change of our attitude towards the circumstances. Either way, everything in our life is subject to change.

Your thoughts will determine your imagination.

Your imagination will determine your choices.

Your choices will determine your destiny.

Make plans today to find out God's thoughts on your issue. Then begin to align your thoughts to His thoughts and your words to His words. Feelings were always meant to follow your faith- never lead.

When you align your thoughts with His thoughts and your words with His words everything else will begin to line up and produce a single mindedness.

Single mindedness is what finalizes and establishes your faith in the heavens. The hand of God is now free to move in your direction!

For more information regarding
Products, Crusade Schedule or Booking:

Billy Burke World Outreach
PO Box 25441
Tampa, FL 33622

1-888-7-HEALED
www.billyburke.org